LET FEAR GO

A guide to help you respond
to life's challenges in a new way
by embracing a FEARLESS mindset.

Lamar Dixon

LEGAL DISCLAIMER

Lamar Dixon © Copyright 2017 - All rights reserved.

In no way is it legal to reproduce, duplicate, or transmit any part of this document by either electronic means or printed format. Recording of this publication is strictly prohibited, and any storage of this document is not allowed unless with written permission from the publisher. All rights reserved.

The information provided herein is stated to be truthful and consistent, in that any liability, regarding inattention or otherwise, by any usage or abuse of any policies, processes, or directions contained within is the solitary and utter responsibility of the recipient reader. Under no circumstances will any legal responsibility or blame be held against the publisher for any reparation, damages, or monetary loss due to the information herein, either directly or indirectly.

Respective authors own all copyrights not held by the publisher. The information herein is offered for informational purposes solely and is universal as so. The presentation of the information is without a contract or any guarantee assurance.

The trademarks used are without any consent, and the publication of the trademark is without permission or backing by the trademark owner. All trademarks and brands within this book are for clarifying purposes only and are then owned by the owners themselves, not affiliated with this document.

Disclaimer and Terms of Use: The Author and Publisher have strived to be as accurate and complete as possible in the creation of this book, notwithstanding the fact that he does not warrant or represent at any time that the contents within are accurate due to the rapidly changing nature of the Internet. While all attempts have been made to verify information provided in this publication, the Author and Publisher assumes no responsibility for errors, omissions, or contrary interpretation of the subject matter herein.

Any perceived slights of specific persons, peoples, or organizations are unintentional. In practical advice books, like anything else in life, there are no guarantees of results. Readers are cautioned to rely on their judgment about their individual circumstances and act accordingly.

This book is not intended for use as a source of legal, medical, business, accounting or financial advice. All readers are advised to seek services of competent professionals in the legal, medical, business, accounting, and finance fields.

Dedication

I dedicate this book to my family and friends.

To my children, nieces, and nephews: Mar, Ari, Aiyanna, Cyrus, Christian, Maya, Kylee, Tye, Amir, Issaiah, Khalee, Zay, Leyah and Luke; I love you!

To my Mom, LaJuana, Ty and Sharmaine: It's incredible how two words that mean so much can seem so diminutive. If I could show you how much your existence in my life means to me, the simple phrase of 'thank you' would pale and diminish in the sheer enormity of the gratitude I owe.

CONTENTS

Introduction 1

Chapter One
Has Your World Lost Its Savor? 3

Chapter Two
How To Live Without Fear - An Easy Way To Start Today 5

Chapter Three
How To Turn Fears Into Fuel 9

Chapter Four
Fear Is Your Best Friend 13

Chapter Five
Steps Of Faith 17

Chapter Six
The Power Of Self-Belief 21

Chapter Seven
Hope Will Get You Through Anything 29

Chapter Eight
What Are PTSD Symptoms? 33

Chapter Nine
Let Fear Go – Personal Anecdote 39

Conclusion 51

INTRODUCTION

Congratulations and thank you for buying the book **"Let Fear Go."**
This book is about helping you respond to life's challenges in a new way by embracing a FEARLESS mindset. By doing this, you will open yourself up to opportunities that can lead you to master your life!

LETTING GO

We hold on to fear even after the moment has passed. What happens to us stays with us, until we make a conscious effort to let go. When we tense up in life, it could be because of a past fear and not just the moment we are in. Fear can come from any minute in your past. When something in our life makes us feel afraid, it can stay with us. We can carry this feeling always. It can spring up when we least expect it, for it is attached to our emotions and thoughts. It can be connected to our expectations of the moment we are in.

At some point in your past, were you faced with something that made you afraid? It could be from such an early stage as your childhood or it could be more recent. Our emotions can stay with us until we hear from them, especially fear; for one of its components is the fear of something happening again. We may not realize how it affects us, but it does. To let go, you have to see that where you are, who you are, and that this moment you are in, is safe. No matter what, believe that you are safe, even if you try to argue otherwise, because you can only benefit from this, no matter the circumstances.

When we take matters into our own hands and start seeing life as something to be enjoyed, embraced and loved, we let go of fear. No matter its origins, fear will no longer have a home in us. Fear can feel like it controls us, but we can, at any moment, let it go because it only manifests if we let it. Believe that fear is a component from your past, that it is no longer beneficial to you. No matter what the future may bring, fear has no place in it.

Have you ever felt fear or anxiety take over your life? If you have, then you will know what a vicious cycle that can be. By changing your mindset, you can learn to become the master of fear, rid yourself of negative self-talk and thus live a life of joy. Sometimes it's not so simple unless, you know an easy way to get started, which you will learn in this guide.

CHAPTER ONE
HAS YOUR WORLD LOST ITS SAVOR?

Disappointment, hopelessness and despair are some of the emotions that may cause us to believe our world has lost its flavor. Life was meant to be filled with beauty, wonder and the magnificence of what could be; a likely cause of our natural instinct to fight so hard to survive. Way down deep, we remember what we believed when we began the journey, when we knew this was true.

For most, it is lost when we believed in people or outcomes that were important to us and a different conclusion was the final result. If the pain is deep enough, we may momentarily park our ability to discern truth to find something or someone to sooth the pain. Unfortunately, it is fairly normal to try to rebuild the same emotions or ideas that just left us bereft and in pain, usually with the same kind of people. It is akin to entering a fun house at the carnival; the same things thrill us, scare us or amuse us. It is our comfort zone. Only the surroundings or identity of the people has changed, when the best prescription for the pain was a change occurring within ourselves or an adjustment to our perceptions.

We begin the revolving door of painful or abusive relationships which can occur with anyone we establish a connection with. We do this by seeking the same kind of people with the same character flaws to fill the same emptiness in our lives, then by responding in the same manner. It is a repeat pattern that alters the course of our destiny. We begin this pattern when we don't take sufficient time to really look at what caused the pain or disappointment the first time, opting to temporarily escape. That temporary path frequently becomes the road we travel on for the duration.

It doesn't have to be this way. We can remember our dreams and what we believed to be truth if we are willing to refuse to enter that revolving door again, willing to park the pain at the door and let go. Letting go means letting go of the people who support the pain process; oddly enough, we are more comfortable with them than starting over. We somehow imagine it to be less painful than dealing with the real cause.

The real cause is our willingness to accept less than our dream supports, to step aside and excuse the inexcusable, our unwillingness to allow others to refuse to be responsible for their behavior or our unwillingness to acknowledge that we simply expected more than the situation could deliver. Many times, this is because we misread the real intentions of those who were part of the pain or loss.

To be truly discerning we must be willing to look closely and without emotion at the people or situations that cause us distress, without any attachment to the outcome. In that state of mind, we find truth. The greatest hurdle may be in accepting that it is the truth. It is necessary to participate in our own success by doing so. The truth is, what we see is what we are going to get. Is it enough to support the dream?

CHAPTER TWO
HOW TO LIVE WITHOUT FEAR - AN EASY WAY TO START TODAY

Have you ever felt fear or anxiety take over your life? If you have, then you will know what a vicious cycle that can be. By changing your mindset, you can learn to become the master of fear, rid yourself of negative self-talk and thus, live a life of joy.

Yet, it can be a problem if you find yourself in a situation where fear is out of control or you are in an anxious state or suffering panic attacks. Changing your mindset isn't so simple. There is an easy way to help shift your energy so you can change your mindset. By the end of this report, you will know exactly what that is.

In the movie, National Treasure, the heroes found themselves in a situation where the "villains" had the upper hand. If they tried to take on the "enemy" at that point, it would have been futile, even making the situation worse. Instead, the heroes do what they can until they have the upper hand. (If you haven't seen National Treasure, I am sure you can think of a movie with a similar synopsis.)

In the same way, before taking any action, it is often best to wait until you are in a better frame of mind. Wait until you have the upper hand. One of the first steps to master fear is not to be frightened of it; which sounds silly in a way. Although many people do fear it. By simply allowing yourself to feel it, fear will pass through you quickly. Perhaps even quicker than you realize.

Here is an exercise to help you achieve that. Actually, you can use this for any "negative" emotion.

Get yourself as comfortable as possible and close your eyes. It doesn't matter whether you are sitting up or lying down. Simply choose which is best for you. Imagine yourself standing in front of a dark pool. That pool represents the fear you are experiencing. Count to three and jump in. Yes, you are going to immerse yourself in it. (If it helps, you can imagine someone who is willing to take the jump with you, holding your hand.) As you swim toward the bottom of the pool allow yourself to experience the fear in its fullness. Don't be too hard on yourself, simply allow yourself to experience it as best as you can. Of course, the more you allow yourself to experience it, the quicker it passes. At first, there may be resistance, but that's OK. Swim deeper and deeper into the feeling.

Then see a bright light at the bottom of the pool, swim towards it. As you do, you will feel yourself getting lighter and lighter. When you reach the bright light, you will see that pool of fear you were swimming through was nothing more than an illusion. You will feel better and the fear will have gone. (If for some reason it hasn't gone through the exercise again. It is probably because you weren't allowing yourself to experience the feeling fully.)

But, what happens when fear has moved onto anxiety and panic attacks. I wouldn't recommend doing the exercise above in a heightened state. The grip of fear will be extremely strong and the "fight or flight" will have kicked in. It could be overwhelming. So, is there anything you can do?

Yes! absolutely. Unlike the scenario above, it is more of a get out of there fast situation. The following step alone is not enough to rid yourself of anxiety. What it will do is bring the anxiety down. By bringing the anxiety down, you are then in a position to use the various cognitive re-training tools. From personal and professional experience, this little trick works a treat! The part of the brain that triggers panic attacks is also the side of the brain that is used for working out complex math problems. Don't worry, I'm not suggesting you start doing calculus!

It is really an easy thing to remember, and even children can use it. All you do is count by 17's. The trick is to do it is in your mind. No pen and paper. If the anxiety is extremely high, it may be a while before you get past 17! But keep going until you feel calmer. The further you count, the more relaxed you will feel. Speaking from personal experience; whenever I use this tool, I can actually feel myself "coming down" from the heightened state. Then, when you have control of the anxiety, you can then start shifting your mindset. (Of course, you can use this technique for anything to help break an unwanted cycle.) This simple tool is incredible.

The mind is powerful and by mastering fears, we truly can live a life of joy.

CHAPTER THREE
HOW TO TURN FEARS INTO FUEL

Contrary to the popular belief, it is not just our physical bodies that are results of evolution. Likewise, it is also our minds; our psychology and our consciousness have been shaped by the world that we evolved in, and that is where a lot of our most unusual behaviors come from.

In the past, our ancestors lived in an extremely dangerous, hazardous and hostile environment where they needed to pay attention to constant potential danger signs and avoid any possible risks. Based on Charles Darwin's theory of the survival for the fittest, only the genes and psychological traits that made us most likely to survive were passed along from generation to generation.

Even though it's thousands, if not millions years later, we still have this nature of risk aversion and that's why it's our default to survive, not to thrive.

It is most people's default to remain in the status quo, instead of disrupting the old model to build new better ones.

It is most people's default to stay in the comfort zone of mediocrity, instead of pushing themselves to be comfortable with the uncomfortable, and pursue the growth zone. It is most people's default to move themselves away from fear instead of facing fear eye-to-eye and lean towards their edges.

WHY ARE WE SO AFRAID OF UNCERTAINTY?

Well, imagine that you were living in an era back in the Stone Age. You were out in the wild, looking at the silhouette of some kind of animal sitting on the horizon. You weren't too sure if that silhouette is of a lion or some kind of kitten, so what do you do? The most pertinent solution in order to survive was to assume the worst. So, it was natural for us to assume it's a fierce, dangerous, life-threatening lion, so we try to freeze, fight or run away. Those who took chances were basically idiots, who were most likely to get eaten and fail to pass on their genes to the next generation.

This was a smart move in the past, but not anymore in today's world. The chances of being eaten by wild animals alive are not even comparable to regular car accidents. Your living environment has changed. Your circumstances have changed. Your biggest threat to your life has changed.

Nowadays, it is problems like obesity, debts, divorces, interpersonal conflicts, careers, happiness and fulfillment issues that bother us the most.

While our biggest "enemies" have changed, our biological nature hasn't evolved much, and it's sabotaging your success in the modern world.

SO, HERE'S THE DEAL.

While it's unfortunate that the human biology and psychology have still remained back in the days, we still have this personal power and a short window of opportunity to choose how we perceive and respond to certain things. We can succumb ourselves to our fears, anxieties, and imaginative worries, OR we can observe our own emotions, remain calm and cool, and be assured that we're not actually in physical danger and there's nothing to be afraid of. In other words, it's our choice to assess any situations with our intelligence, claim ownership of our stressful feelings, and take action to transform our psychology into a more empowering state.

Be objective about the circumstances.

Let your excuses pop up and have a laugh at these mindless noises.

Take massive imperfect action immediately because you're safe and secure, and action cures all.

That's exactly how you turn fears into fuels.

> "I think therefore I am."

CHAPTER FOUR
FEAR IS YOUR BEST FRIEND

A MIND-MADE ILLUSION

In a civilized society, fear impairs the lives of many who but into the notion think that fear is real. It was the French philosopher René Descartes who said, "I think therefore I am." In other words, if there are thoughts, there must be a thinker behind the thoughts. Moreover, many people unknowingly buy into the false premise "If I think fearful thoughts, they must be true."

You've heard that fear is an illusion created in the mind. A great deal of what we fear rarely comes to fruition, yet fear seems to predominate our thought landscape. Since fear is a survival instinct which alerts us to impending danger, it only becomes a threat when our thoughts become stuck in a repetitive cycle. When fear rules your life, you are at the mercy of the emotion.

TRANSFORMING FEAR

How can we reframe fear to view it as friend rather than a foe? First, appreciate that fear is a feedback mechanism alerting you to forward progress. You are stepping out of your comfort zone and moving into the unchartered territory. Rather than oppose fear, embrace it by viewing it as an opportunity to gain new insights as you advance onward. Embrace the fear by observing it as part of the process of evolving. Many people view fear as a brick wall, while others see it as an opportunity to overcome it.

Fear is your best friend since it inspires a call to action. It advises us to avoid that which is deleterious and take affirmative action. Take for example, the fear of public speaking which is considered one of people's greatest fears. The American comedian, Jerry Seinfeld offers us the following comedic observation, "According to most studies, people's number one fear is public speaking. Number two is death. Death is number two. Does that sound right? This means to the average person, if you go to a funeral, you're better off in the casket than doing the eulogy."

In this instance, fear forces us to brush up on our speaking skills through rehearsal. Rather than appearing incompetent, fear forces us to show up prepared. As we overcome fear, we not only build character and inner strength, we overcome an impediment on our path to victory. Therefore, fear becomes a great teacher since it provides us with the experience before the lesson.

RECONNECTING TO THE PRESENT MOMENT

Moreover, fear reminds us to stay connected to the present moment. Given that fear is a future occurrence, it allows us to reconnect back to the present moment when our minds wander into the future. We are reminded that all we ever have is contained within the perfection of this moment. There is no need to worry or fear a future which seldom arrives as we hope for. Therefore, fear reminds us to let go of the incessant thoughts of an anticipated tomorrow.

It must be stated that we cannot eliminate fear from our lives, not in the way many people believe. We can turn down the volume on fear by not becoming a slave to it. Susan Jeffers' acclaimed self-help book, Feel the Fear and Do It Anyway is an appropriate axiom for learning to befriend fear. When faced with the prospect of taming our worries, we are reminded that fear helps us sharpen the sword, as it were, by making better decisions in lieu of perceived danger. We must have our wits about us as we confront our fears.

Your response to fear provides you with a glimpse into your deeper psyche. Are you continually running away from fear or brave enough to face it head on? Fear is a call toward inner growth and inner freedom. Running away from your fears makes them grow stronger until they overwhelm you. Rather than oppose your doubts, approach them with compassion and an open heart. Forgive yourself and others who may have contributed towards your fears.

You might be surprised to learn that a number of our fears are passed down through generations. Wars and hatred stem from the paralysis of fear. First, we fear that which we do not understand, then we ultimately go to war with it.

Ultimately you have a choice - to make peace with fear or allow it to control your life. Hopefully, I've provided you with some valid points to choose the former. Transcending fear is liberating since it frees you from the self-imposed fortress, which is the illusory mind of fear.

"Feel the Fear and Do It Anyway"

CHAPTER FIVE
STEPS OF FAITH

Faith is often seen as a uniquely religious concept. While most often considered a spiritual force, it is not reserved for religious purposes. When we take a step in faith, we are using an internal power that has the potential to change everything.

We should use it wisely.

Recently, I was surfing through my cable selections, I happened upon one of those now ubiquitous weight loss programs which focus on extremely obese people and their struggle to lose weight. The show featured a woman who, with evidence of before and after photos, demonstrated that before she had children, she was young and svelte. After giving birth, her busy life working and caring for her children lead to gaining a pound here and there. Eventually she was so big, a film crew became interested in her. She blamed her obesity on having children.

I do not discount the weight women gain in pregnancy, nor do I minimize the effort required to lose that weight after childbirth. My point is that to blame her obesity on having children completely discounts the fifteen or twenty years of emotions, attitudes and behaviors that are more likely the cause of her obesity. She has placed herself in a kind of prison, the bars of which are created by her own belief.

When she acts on that belief, she is, in a very powerful way, taking a step of faith. Faith does not necessarily imply God at the other end of it. Certainly, adhering to religious principals is an act of faith, but faith and religion are two different things. Faith is a human tool that we all use. Every time we act or react because we believe something, we are stepping in faith. Tightrope walkers, for example, step out onto the rope believing that they can and will cross the rope safely. Their belief is well-founded on the hours of practice they have had, but every tightrope walker is aware of the potential danger of falling. They simply do not believe that they will fall. If they believed that they were going to fall, they would never step out onto the rope.

The unfortunate thing for a lot of religious folks is that they associate faith with God or a miracle from God and leave it at that. There is a very real reason why many people ask God for a miracle and never get it. Faith itself is the miracle they are waiting for. When we learn to use faith appropriately, we unleash a power, call it spiritual if you like, that enables us to achieve our goals and aspirations.

When we are willing to take risks, however we define them; it is because we believe something is either possible or impossible. The trick is discerning the difference between what we know to be true and what we think or feel is true.

Some people think you need courage to take risks. That is not true. You need courage to face danger. You need faith to take risks. Risk and danger are two different things, and so are faith and courage. It takes courage to run into a burning building to save a child. It takes faith to believe you can do it at all.

Every time I step in front of an audience, I act in faith believing that the audience will benefit from my speech, enjoy my performance, and my client will consider my fee to be money well spent. It is like walking out on a tightrope. I have plenty of practice, but the possibility of my failing is there. So, public speaking is a kind of a risk I am willing to take.

It is easy to see faith involved in actively taking risks. When we decide to not do something, it is often because we believe that we will fail. In some cases, that is good. I will never step out on a tightrope, since I am absolutely convinced I would fall off. That being said, what achievable goals or dreams am I avoiding simply because I have an unfounded, even irrational belief in failure?

If there is an aspect of our lives with which we are growing uncomfortable, if anything at all is going to change, we need to pay attention to what it is we believe about it. Once we clear up what we believe about the things we would like to change, the most formidable obstacles are gone.

It may sound like hocus pocus, psychobabble or even new age religion but the truth is that we act as a result of what we believe. We live our lives doing some things, avoiding others, and likely wishing we could someday still do others; all because of what we believe about the world, about other people, and about ourselves and yes, even what we believe about God. Those beliefs may or may not be factual, but we make them real to us.

We all have a spiritual side to our lives. It is that part of us that helps us cope with the unknown and, within the context of our own lives, the unknowable. Science gnaws away at the unknown but any honest scientist will admit that there is a lot we do not know. Until we know absolutely everything that is knowable, we will continue to take steps of faith, acting or not acting based on what we believe to be true.

So, we are all stuck with faith of one sort or another. Faith is not something you can create, build up or muster, but it is a natural part of being human. We act on it every day. Along our journey to find happiness, balance and purpose in life, we would do well to consider what it is we believe about every situation, condition or obstacle we face.

"Fear is your best friend since it inspires a call to action."

CHAPTER SIX
THE POWER OF SELF-BELIEF

Too many people have let themselves become dependent on others and as a result of this, they no longer believe in their own power to get things done or are simply out of touch with that side of themselves. When you lack confidence in your own power to get things done, you will find yourself unhappy, unsuccessful and desperate for a way out. Unfortunately, most normal people, not seeing any easy way out, will give in and settle for a life of dependency, simply because it's easier. It's amazing how people would rather settle for mediocrity and inferiority than make a little extra effort to rediscover their independence.

The one thing I have learned, which we need to get clear in our minds is that, it is not the situations we are facing that make us feel bad; it is the way we choose to view them that makes us feel as bad as we do. When we spend our lives viewing the world through these grey tinted glasses, what happens is we eventually lose confidence and develop the classic "inferiority complex." The world is full of these so-called "problems" and it is only human nature to focus on them, hence giving them more power than they deserve. In order to develop your self-belief, you must first stop focusing on your problems, which incidentally, may not be "problems" when looked at from a different perspective.

Change your attitude towards life and the fabric of your existence changes. The famous psychologist, Dr. Carl Menninger once said, "Attitudes are more important than facts." I wholeheartedly agree with that statement purely because, with the right attitude, anyone can make something of themselves. For example, take two unemployed men going for the same job position, one who believes in himself and is confident of getting the job; and the other who has zero confidence and self-belief. Despite them both being equally qualified, the man with self-belief is hired. Why? Well, because when you believe in yourself; your subconscious mind floods your conscious mind with positive thoughts, ideas and solutions; whereas if you have no confidence in yourself, you get nothing except negative thoughts and blankness. Consequently, the interviewer saw the confident man's eagerness and belief in his own ability, and wanted him on his team.

Believe in yourself and don't beat yourself up when you make mistakes, as mistakes are our Teachers and nobody who did anything of note did it without making mistakes. Your attitude determines what your life will have to offer; don't make the mistake of allowing your circumstances to determine your attitude otherwise, you will never grow and must surely settle for a life of mediocrity. You would be amazed at how many people sabotage their life and its circumstances and outcomes due to a lack of self-belief.

Millions of people every day permit others to create doubt in their ability to accomplish their goals, cause them to feel insecure and unworthy and generally, contribute to the poor value of their mental state and therefore, often the quality of their life in general. Why is this?

LOTS OF REASONS BUT HERE ARE A FEW TO CONSIDER.

Self-belief is nothing more than confidence in who you are, what you believe, and how you feel. It doesn't mean you are always right in these mindsets, but as long as you believe them and act accordingly, they will impact your thoughts, attitudes and life. We could use some of history's most famous bad people as an example - they were wrong in their attitudes, but because they believed in them and thought they were right they behaved accordingly and therefore had a great deal of negative influence on the world. I could also give you examples of some of the world's best people who had the same confidence in their beliefs and values and had tremendous positive influence on the world in general. The rules for both were the same - believe in yourself, and the outcomes will mirror your beliefs.

Do you have steadfast belief in yourself, your life purpose, your actions and decisions, your behavior? If so, I would have to ask - are the outcomes for the people in your life - family, friends, customers, employees or strangers - positive or negative?

Self-belief, when real and passionate, will lead to congruence between your thoughts and actions and therefore, your outcomes and circumstances. When self- belief is grounded in integrity, knowledge and respect for your higher self, it will push you towards your dreams, goals and desires. When self-belief is honored in all ways, it will propel you into a future that you dream will one day be true for you. In essence, your dreams are really only as possible as your belief in them. So, if your dreams are not a reality yet - consider - that maybe your-self-belief needs some serious work - from the inside-out.

When you allow appearances and external conditions to influence your self-belief, you will almost always fall short of your dreams and desires. So, please get this - if you want the future you envision for yourself to become a reality one day - start focusing on the development, improvement, enhancement and confidence in who you are, who you are becoming and who you are capable of becoming. Easy task? Not at all. But worth the effort, time, work and patience? A resounding YES!!

"In the province of the mind, what one believes to be true either is true or becomes true." John Lilly. The mind is an incredibly powerful thing. If you believe (and I mean truly believe), you can do something then, your subconscious will work to make it fact.

You believe in your career and in yourself, or you wouldn't be where you are now. But, do you have that internal negative voice sometimes? You know the one that undermines your positive beliefs, tries to tell that you won't make it to the next level up, that you will never achieve a healthy work/life balance or that you're no good at a particular area of your work? If you feed your subconscious negative things about yourself and your career, it will look for ways to prove that you are right. And so, your beliefs will be constantly reinforced and may ultimately actually become fact. Let's see what we can do about that.

What I'd like you to do for a moment is concentrate on your main goal for your career. Close your eyes and take yourself forward to the time when you have achieved it, when your career (and accordingly, your lifestyle) is everything you want it to be. Stay there for a minute or two and really drink it in. Take note of what you can see, hear and feel.

ASK YOURSELF:

- What strengths did I have back when I was planning to get here, which enabled me to get to this point?

Now, come back to the present and keep hold of those positive thoughts.

We all hold Empowering Beliefs. These are the beliefs which empower us to move forwards towards our goals. Some of them, we know and can list straight away. Others may surprise us when we encourage our subconscious to come forward with them. All of them are extremely powerful and make a huge difference to the outcome of all our endeavors.

When you express an Empowering Belief, the sentence would typically start 'I am...' or 'I can...'

Basing your list on your answer to the bullet pointed question above, write down now 5 Empowering Beliefs you have about your career. What are its strengths? What does it do for you? What do you love about it? 'It is... what?' 'It can... what?' 'It does... what?'

Once again basing your list on your answer to the question, write down now 5 Empowering Beliefs you have about yourself which will enable you to get your career to where you want it to be. 'I am...?' 'I can...? 'I'm great at...?' 'My XYZ skills are superb.' Don't worry if you think it might sound big-headed to anyone else. What's important is that you believe that you have this strength, ability or knowledge.

WRITE 5 EMPOWERING BELIEFS ABOUT YOURSELF:

1. _____

2. _____

3. _____

4. _____

5. _____

That's a great start!

Now, commit to doing something over the next couple of weeks. Every day, add at least one new Empowering Belief to your two lists. Your goal is to end up in 2 weeks time with at least 10

Empowering Beliefs about your career and at least 10 Empowering Beliefs about you.

SO EACH DAY ASK YOURSELF: 'WHAT ELSE?'

Ask other people what they think. Ask colleagues, clients, friends and family. When someone else gives you some positive feedback, accept that they wouldnot say it, unless it was true. So, you can easily take that on as a belief of your own - right?

Keep your lists where you can access them easily and often, particularly if you are having a 'wobble moment.' This is really powerful stuff and can cause a mental shift that will take you shooting forwards. Please note; I am not saying that empowering beliefs alone will make things happen. But, if you accept and believe all the positive things about your current and future career and about yourself, you will actually go out there and take the action necessary to make it happen! What's the alternative?

"Hope is the belief things will work, especially when it seems otherwise."

CHAPTER SEVEN
HOPE WILL GET YOU THROUGH ANYTHING

Life is full of twists and turns; it's easy to become despondent. Obstacles and adversities show up unexpectedly and we find ourselves out of our comfort zone.

People say life is unfair? I presume they're referring to life being unfavorable when things don't go as planned.

Surely, we're intelligent enough to know, we don't always get what we want. Sorry to rain on your parade. Regardless, one thing that's helped me remain optimistic is that not everything will go as planned and that's okay. In fact, not getting what I want is often a good thing, since there's often something greater on the horizon to fill its place.

We must accept life will be full of obstacles, road blocks, negative emotions and circumstances that will derail our best-laid plans. Knowing this should remove the burden; life is not pure sailing, but an adventure full of valleys and victories.

If you fear, "what could go wrong next," you place an unnecessary burden on your shoulders while dreading the worst.

If you adopt a hopeful and optimistic heart, you can breathe easier and expect a more pleasant future.

HOPE HAS WHAT IT TAKES

Hope is more valuable than we give it credit for. It's a soft burning flame, unable to be extinguished and capable of enduring any conditions. Hope has what it takes to get you through anything. People usually consider hope among the most wondrous of gifts: it keeps us going when we want to quit and makes possible victories that seem unattainable. Hope is the belief things will work, especially when it seems otherwise. It helps you stay calm and peaceful when something less than desirable emerges.

Hope believes you will get through it.

Hope remembers the times you made it through.

Hope teams with faith and believes in the impossible.

EMOTIONAL UPHEAVAL

When times are tough, our emotions are intensified and not symbolic of whom we are. When the boss tells you the company is downsizing and your position is terminated, when your son gets expelled from school, your partner decides they don't know if they want to spend the rest of their life with you, and the doctor gives you an adverse health report or your dog's gone missing, then your emotions are in for a roller-coaster ride.

But with hope, your thoughts gravitate toward optimism. We cannot expect life to be smooth sailing. Unexpected conditions arise, not to overwhelm us but to test our inner resolve and awaken us to our true power. Our emotional response in such times is not indicative of our true self. That's because we respond to our external environment instead of staying composed.

LESSONS TO BE LEARNED

Sometimes when a situation is bleak, you're invited to master a lesson greater than you expect. This is when hope will get you through. If you lose your job, there might be a series of experiences during your transition of looking for another job.

You may realize you loathed your previous job and are now more determined to find a career path that makes you happy. Maybe you realize, you want to start your own business instead of working for someone. Consider this something to learn from instead of dwelling on the unfortunate setbacks.

Assuredly, there's a lesson and inner growth contained within your circumstances, even if you can't see it yet. I appreciate the advice from author Jan Frazier in The Freedom of Being: At Ease with What Is, "The reality is that in the interval between the start of hope and when the outcome occurs, you don't know what's going to happen. The ego-mind dislikes not knowing. Feeling hope is a way of avoiding the discomfort of uncertainty."

VISUALIZE A POSITIVE FUTURE

During hard times, do your best to envision a positive future. In fact, what you dwell upon is what you likely will get. Call it positive thinking; though what you hold in your mind is what you will receive. We're the product of our emotions, given that we feel our way through life. If your emotions are fixed on negative aspects, you're likely to attract those situations because of your predominant reactions. The universe reflects what you put out into the ether.

As an example, if I entertain negative thoughts related to not having enough money to pay my bills, I'll see evidence of this echoed in reality. I might notice TV commercial discussing debt prevention or perhaps someone mentions their financial difficulties. If I'm aware, I recognize the warning signs that my thoughts are out of alignment. If I persist with these thoughts, it's likely to materialize because I've willed it into existence, whether I like it or not.

"Scientists have repeatedly demonstrated that changing our perspective and focusing on aspects of the situation that are in our control, can have a hugely beneficial impact on our hope, motivation, and self-esteem," states author Guy Winch in Emotional First Aid: Practical Strategies for Treating Failure, Rejection, Guilt, and Other Everyday Psychological Injuries.

HOW DO YOU SEE YOUR FUTURE DEVELOPING?

Close your eyes for a moment and visualize an optimistic path. It requires work and discipline to create an intentional future, and it can't be achieved overnight. This is because you're likely to slip into your old ways, if you're not mindful of your thoughts.

UNATTACHED TO OUTCOMES

The world is full of people who have overcome incredible hurdles and failures to become successful and happy. They're unattached to outcomes because they appreciate that not everything goes as planned. When one door closes, another opens at the right time, as long as their thoughts are in alignment.

Allow life to weave her mysterious ways by being detaching from outcomes. What appears detrimental at first may simply be laying the groundwork for something greater later. Commit to a life of optimism, irrespective of the circumstances and raise the beacon of hope when times are tough. You can become confident through your willingness to see life from a different viewpoint. The next time something doesn't go as planned, draw on hope and declare, "It'll be alright, I trust for the best in this situation" and chances are, it will turn out as you intend.

Hope will get you through anything, but first, you must create the circumstances for it to flourish, before it sets your world alight.

CHAPTER EIGHT
WHAT ARE PTSD SYMPTOMS?

There are numerous reports of military veterans suffering from Post Traumatic Stress Disorder (PTSD)-like symptoms for over 100 years. Veterans of the US Civil War who suffered emotional problems were diagnosed as being afflicted with "soldier's heart" or "Da Costa's Syndrome" which shares many symptoms like PTSD. Shell shock was a term used to describe the condition of veterans of World War I who seemed emotionally disturbed in a similar fashion. In World War II, these symptoms were classified as "battle fatigue" or "combat fatigue." Other terms used to describe military-related mood disturbances include "nostalgia", "not yet diagnosed nervous", "irritable heart", "effort syndrome", "war neurosis", and "operational exhaustion".

Post-traumatic stress disorder, commonly referred to as PTSD, is an anxiety disorder a person may experience following a traumatic event involving the threat of death or personal injury, causing extreme fear, terror, or hopelessness. Symptoms of PTSD may present as early as within the first month following the traumatic event or as long as several months or years later. It is important for a person with PTSD to be treated by a mental health professional experienced in working with PTSD.

RE-EXPERIENCING THE EVENT

Most people who experience PTSD continue to re-experience the traumatic event that caused their PTSD. The event may be experienced through flashbacks. Flashbacks can be fleeting glimpses of memory or as vivid as watching a movie of the event. Intrusive memories or thoughts are another way the traumatic event is experienced. A person may be unable to control these thoughts. They may surface at any time regardless of the individual's situation or current emotional state. Nightmares of the traumatic event are common and upon waking, the person may experience physical sensations triggered by and associated with the event. They may also awaken experiencing extreme fear and anxiety.

AVOIDANCE AND NUMBNESS

People living with PTSD may try to avoid thinking or talking about the event. Avoidance of people, places, and activities that are reminders of the trauma is also common. Numbness may be experienced in different ways. A person may feel emotionally numb, experience feelings of hopelessness about the future, and have difficulty with memory and concentration. At times, this numbness can lead to social and emotional detachment from friends and family members. In some extreme cases, the person will suppress all memories of the traumatic event.

INCREASED AROUSAL

Symptoms of increased arousal are emotional responses that occur following a traumatic event. Feeling on edge and being easily startled, or frightened can lead to prolonged anxiety, causing sleep difficulties. Some people experience difficulty concentrating on tasks or projects in a variety of settings. Increased anger and irritability are emotions that commonly surface and aid in avoiding emotions related to the traumatic event.

FIVE TREATMENTS FOR POST-TRAUMATIC STRESS DISORDER

There are a variety of good treatments available for post-traumatic stress disorder (PTSD). Dealing with past traumatic events can be difficult and you may tend to keep your feelings to yourself instead of expressing them to others. Talking with a counselor can be helpful.

Treatment for PTSD usually involves a combination of medication and psychotherapy. With this combination of treatments, your symptoms may improve while you are learning to utilize various coping skills to deal with the traumatic event and its effects on your life. There are five basic psychotherapy approaches used in treating PTSD.

COGNITIVE THERAPY

In cognitive therapy, your therapist will assist you in discovering thought patterns related to your trauma and help you identify and challenge ways of thinking, which cause you stress and interfere with healthy living. Your therapist will help you replace your limiting thoughts with thoughts that are less distressing. You will learn ways to cope with feelings like fear, anger, and guilt.

After a traumatic event, you may tend to blame yourself, feel guilt for what occurred or for decisions made. Cognitive therapy helps you understand your thoughts and perspective of the event, reducing unnecessary feelings of guilt.

EXPOSURE THERAPY

Exposure therapy is a behaviorally based technique that helps you safely face what you are frightened of, so you can learn ways to cope more effectively. When you are suffering from PTSD, it is common to be afraid of thoughts, feelings, or situations that remind you of your traumatic event. The goal of exposure therapy is for you to experience less fear about your memories. When processing the trauma in a safe environment with your therapist, you can change how you react to the memories while practicing different ways to relax. It may seem odd to think about stressful things purposefully, but over time, you will learn that you do not have to fear your memories and you will feel less overwhelmed.

EMDR

Eye movement desensitization and reprocessing (EMDR) is another type of therapy used to treat PTSD. It is a combination of exposure therapy and guided eye movements, sounds, and hand taps that help you process traumatic memories. The goal of EMDR, similar to other types of therapy, is to help change how you react to traumatic memories.

GROUP THERAPY

You may find it helpful to talk about your trauma with others who have had similar experiences. In group therapy, you will talk with others who have been through a trauma and have PTSD. Sharing your story, and building relationships with others can help you cope with your memories, emotions, and symptoms, as well as help you build trust and self-confidence.

MEDICATION

There are varieties of medications that have been used to treat PTSD. They have been shown to be helpful in reducing sadness and worry. When you are depressed, you may not have enough of the chemical called serotonin. Selective serotonin reuptake inhibitors (SSRIs) are a type of antidepressant medication, which increase the serotonin level in your brain. Other types of medications have been successful as well. Talk with your doctor to determine if medication might be helpful for you.

PTSD is very common in those who have served in the armed forces and can occur as the result of any trauma in life. Help is available.

TRAUMA-SENSITIVE YOGA

The long -term symptoms, as well as effects that trauma creates, often reflects post-traumatic stress disorder (PTSD), which is a condition of emotional, as well as mental stress that is persistent, which occurs after a traumatic event. People that are diagnosed with PSTD can relieve themselves from the event through intrusive memories, flashbacks, as well as nightmares: in a nutshell, avoiding anything that reminds them of the trauma. Many people are suffering from this situation today. The good news is that yoga can help bring relieve to people suffering from this.

When someone is just recovering from emotional trauma, health professionals recommends that the person should engage in some healthy behaviors, in order to enhance your ability to cope with excessive stress. In addition to performing proper rest, nutrition, as well as avoiding drugs and alcohol, it is suggestted that some relaxation techniques should be considered in this regard. However, if we consider the effects of trauma, then we can fully understand why relaxation might not come easily to people who are suffering from PSTD. This kind of condition is when trauma-sensitive yoga can be employed.

ASSOCIATION THROUGH MEDITATION

Students can reconnect easily to themselves, as well as in the present environment, and in a safe environment through trauma-sensitive yoga. There are some meditation techniques that encourage yoga students to acknowledge thoughts as well as feelings, which arise without having the pressure to react to them.

CHAPTER NINE
LET FEAR GO – PERSONAL ANECDOTE

December 15th, 2011, I was honorably discharged from the United States Air Force for failing my physical fitness test seven times. Since the age of 18, all I knew for the last fourteen years, three months and two days was serving my country. After being stationed in Virginia, Qatar, Turkey, and Italy, we were being stationed (moving) to my mother's two-bedroom apartment in Philadelphia with daughter Maya and my son Lamar Jr.

With my younger brother's truck which I borrowed and no income, I hit the ground running. The first step was to enroll Maya and Lamar in school, and I registered to take courses at the Community College of Philadelphia (CCP). Next, I needed to get a job. I applied for 20 jobs a day that matched my qualifications. My thoughts were "with my experience; I'll get any job." I was wrong. With every interview, I heard the same line; "You have the experience, but you don't have the education. I'm sorry Mr. Dixon." Over the next four months, I heard that line repeatedly. It was hard to deal with rejection. There was no choice, but to apply for government assistance. It was my lowest point. I was trapped in fear, anxiety, and depression.

In April 2012, things started to change upward. I reconnected with an old friend (that eventually became my wife), I was awarded Veteran's compensation for my injuries from military service, my younger brother bought a home for us to live in (We had to pay rent of course) and in May 2012, I started taking classes at CCP. Honestly, the only reason I enrolled was to use my military benefits and receive a monthly stipend. I probably ranked in the lower 20 percent of my graduating High School class, so it was tough gearing up for college after 14 years. The first semester was rough. I was 33 years old in classes with kids that were between the ages of 18 and 20. While I am trying to focus on learning algebra, they're in the back talking about trends and texting. It was a tough adjustment, but I made it through with a 3.21 GPA and I started to have a feeling of gratification.

After the first semester, I was inducted into the Alpha Beta Gamma Honor Society. It was a great feeling, but I wasn't satisfied. With every milestone, I started to compare my life to my friends and family. I was/am very happy and excited for them, but I felt that I was so far behind. They had multiple homes, cars, and degrees and at this point, I felt like my life was a failure. I continued to take classes at CCP until December 2013, when I graduated with an Associate's Degree in Management of Computer Information Technology.

"My only competition is with who I was yesterday"

The day after graduation, I woke up and had a sudden revelation. I realized that I that my only competition is with who I was yesterday. Once I comprehended this, my life changed. I stopped seeking the approval of others, I stop comparing myself to others and I stop believing I was a failure. That day, I understood my path is just that, MY PATH. I kept repeating "My only competition is with who I was yesterday." I wrote it everywhere; Facebook, Instagram, and on post it notes. I had to keep reminding myself.

In January 2014, I started working at Office Depot as a supply clerk on the weekends, and I transferred to my dream college, Temple University. Making $9.10 an hour working at Office Depot isn't where I expected to be. I always thought I would be one of those guys walking super-fast around Center City Philadelphia with a fancy suit, a cup of coffee in my hand and a newspaper in the other. At the time, my wife had birthed our son Luke and I needed the extra income for his daycare. I thank God for the job and the experience. It humbled me and altered my way thinking that I deserved a $100,000 job for my 14 years of service. I learned quickly nothing is given, everything is earned. I worked there for six months. It was a 45-minute commute, so I always arrived 30 minutes early for my shift. While there, I worked my tail off. I didn't care what I had to do. All I knew was, I wanted to be the best at it. I worked there, while being enrolled in five courses at Temple. I remember being so excited to start class.

As an adolescent, I grew up in North Philadelphia and visited the campus many times. I loved every minute of it! I would sneak into McGonigle Hall to see Eddie Jones, Lynn Grier or Aaron McKie do basketball shooting drills or go meet my good friend Ihsan who attended there. We would run a full court game with the students. It was always intense and good competition. I couldn't wait to wear the "Cherry and White." The first semester at Temple was a good time. I met so many students, fellow veterans and faculty members. It was inspiring to be around so many people that were striving to be successful, and valuable to any company that hired them.

At times, I doubted myself and thought I didn't deserve to be here. I thought I wasn't smart enough and I was too old, but I kept pushing. After the first semester, I received an invitation for an honor society. Again, here is a point in my life where I should be proud and I didn't enjoy the moment. I didn't tell anyone about it, because I didn't think they would excite as I was. I had too many ups and downs, and at this point, I needed to get help.

I decided to visit the Philadelphia VA Medical Center, so they can assess my temperament. After being evaluated, I was diagnosed with post-traumatic stress disorder or PTSD. I never would have thought that I had it. To me, I always laughed and had fun, but to my family I was always on edge. If we scheduled something and a person was late, I would be full of rage! My wife was late picking me up from the train station, and I was pissed; my brother and his family was always late to gatherings, and I was pissed; I went on a family vacation with my mom and yelled at her, because I waited several hours for her and the family to get ready (I'm sorry Mom); but I was pissed. I had to get help.

I arrived for the assessment and the physician was 45 minutes late for the session. I lost it. I told him he was unprofessional and yelled at him for wasting my time (I was such a jerk). During the assessment, the physician asked me various questions such as; how do you sleep? Where do I sit in class? How are you out in public? My answers were; "I never sleep in my bed; I sleep on the couch every night in case there is a noise. I always sit in the back of the class, so no one can sneak behind me and I usually go food shopping 6:15 am to avoid people and long lines and I'll go see a movie at 10:30 am to avoid a crowded area." After hearing myself answer these questions, I found myself living in a shell. I had the same routine for three years. I realized, I was punishing myself for not being where I wanted to be in life and I lost myself. I lived in fear and wasn't enjoying the journey.

I knew that to get my mind under control, I would have to devise a plan. So, I composed a list of things that triggered my anger, my fears and my goals for the next two years.

ANGER LIST
- Repeating something more than three times.
- Motorists driving slow.
- Individuals being late for anything that's scheduled
- Leaving the military

GOALS
- Buy a new home
- Start a scholarship
- Plan a trip
- Be the guy with a fancy job walking fast around center city with a cup of coffee.
- Graduate from Temple University

I made these lists and prepared a two-year plan for each one of them. I wanted to gain control of my thoughts and actions. Writing down my fears, triggers and goals helped me visualize what was going on and what I wanted to achieve in the next two years. I reaized, without a plan, how will you reach your destination?

After writing my anger list, I knew I had to work on being patient. I made sure that I left 15 minutes earlier for every planned appointment, to avoid motorists driving slowly. If a person was late, I'll give them a ten-minute grace period, and then I'll leave depending on the situation. By being in the military, it was embedded in my mind that "if you're early; you're on time and if you're on time; you're late!" It took me three years to realize those rules don't apply in the civilian world.

"The best years of your life are the ones in which you decide your problems are your own. You do not blame them on your mother, the ecology, or the president. You realize that you control your own destiny."
– Albert Ellis

Looking at my fear list I laughed. Instantly, I knew that just because I took a little longer than others doesn't mean I failed. I had to let it go. I remember when Maya was a little younger, she was afraid of bugs and I would say "stop running; you're bigger than that". I'm bigger than my fears and it was time to face them. My fears became my affirmations that I would declare over my life. Every day, I would say; I will be successful, I am smart enough, my only competition is with whom I was yesterday and I will be a great husband.

Every time I would review my goals, my skin would tingle and I had the biggest smile. I felt like I could reach out and grab them. When I started this two-year goals list, I made sure that they were SMART; Specific, Measurable, Attainable, Realistic and Time-based. To acquire the house and the car, I would have to work on my credit. After assessing my report, I made sure the balance of every credit card was under 30% of credit utilization. Just doing this helped my credit jump up 100 points. My next goal was plan a trip.

Around the time I started planning a trip, I received a couple invitations. One was from my friend Taurian to be a groomsman in his wedding in Mexico. He also invited me to his Air Force retirement ceremony held in Arizona a few months later. The other invitation was from Johnny who was retiring from the Air Force in Florida later that year. After punishing myself for so many years, I was hesitant to commit because I felt as if I didn't deserve to go. It wasn't about me. It was about supporting my friends that has always supported me. I prepared myself psychologically and went to every event and had a good time. I finally enjoyed the moment. Being around good friends was the therapy I needed and it reminded me of whom I used to be.

So, after years of the same routine over and over. I finally came out of my shell and went to Cancun, Chicago, Tuscan and Tampa within six months. Now, it was time for me to choose my career path.

"Choose a job you love, and you will never have to work a day in your life." After leaving Office Depot, I decided to focus on my school work and look for a job that I would enjoy. I was thankful for the opportunity, but my dreams were bigger. For the next two months, I prepared for Temple University's Annual Information Technology Career Fair. Over 30 employers are scheduled to participate such as; Merck, Wal-Mart, Lockheed Martin, QVC and Ernest Young. I worked on my elevator speech, resume and interview questions. If the opportunity knocked, I was going to be ready.

Without a plan, how will you reach your destination?

On this page, I would like you to write down your anger triggers, your fears and most importantly, your goals! This list will allow you to know what your destination is, and you will have a general idea about how you can reach it.

ANGER LIST

- _____
- _____
- _____
- _____
- _____

GOALS

- _____
- _____
- _____
- _____
- _____

I arrived to career fair very equipped with detailed research of every company that was in attendance, copies of my resume and a very sweaty shirt from being so nervous. I circled the room once, and my first stop was at my preferred company. I introduced myself and we conversed for 30 minutes. I was so confident that I would receive a call back for an interview; I didn't speak to any other business. A month later, I received a call back for the interview and a month after that I accepted a role as an intern. I was so excited! But I knew that there were going to be some tough challenges to get hired full time. I accepted the role in November 2014. Then internship didn't start until May 2015.

Fast Forward to May 19th 2015, today is the day I start my internship! At this point, I'm humbled, appreciative and focused. I get up early, ate breakfast and now, I'm having a tough time deciding what to wear on my first day. I think about an Oscar Wilde quote "you can never be overdressed or overeducated." So, I decided to put on my favorite suit and tie. I arrived early, and I noticed that everyone else is dressed casual. The company's motto when it comes to the dress code is "be the real you." This gives employees the flexibility to choose the appropriate attire based on what's happening on any specific day. There are 50 interns and I'm the only one sweating in a suit. After orientation, I met my manager, Scott. Before he even shook my hand, he laughed and said "are you going to wear a suit everyday". He was that type of guy.

I had zero training and was the least experienced among the interns starting in this new information technology role. My only understanding was what I learned from my courses and YouTube. I struggled initially, but Scott pulled me through. He became my mentor and helped me transition from being so military gung-ho to understanding the corporate culture. Some areas in Information Technogly are very customer focus driven. Initially, when I spoke with senior leaders within the company, I did everything but salute. It was always yes sir or no ma'am and some people got offended by it. I had to be more of myself and not a robot. I learned to incorporate my military habits with my own persona. Whenever I assisted any personnel, I would always stand-up to show respect when communicating and if the timing was right, I would slide in a joke just to get the user to smile.

It took time for me to gain business acumen of the environment. I had to learn the different operating systems, what software each section used and how to research ways to solve problems. It took months before I was confident in how I was performing, but I gained trust from leadership and was extended another month past my end date for the internship program and eventually I received an offer for full time employment! It was an amazing feeling! After receiving the offer on a late Friday afternoon, I hung up the phone and stared out the window with my hands on my head and thanked God repeatedly. My grandmother always told me that "If you want to make God laugh then tell him your plans." It's not a job in center city and I'm not wearing a fancy suit every day as I planned. My job is headquartered in Camden, New Jersey. I am grateful, and I don't take this path God paved for granted.

"It's a pretty awesome experience to serve others without expecting anything in return"

Several months after being hired, I closed on a new home and received a promotion. Everything is starting to fall in place. I have a great job, I completed my undergraduate degree, I became a better father and my family was doing well. I felt it was time to give back, so I started a scholarship at the High School I graduated from. It was a great feeling to give back, but I wanted to do more. I founded the Dixon Education Foundation. Our mission is to award scholarships to deserving veterans and students at schools across the country, helping them to finish their education and start successful careers.

I want to be committed to provide opportunities to those who want to learn, improve and succeed. In less than three months, gave one $1000 scholarship. We've also donated time to assist with cleaning parks, preparing 700 book bags to donate to the students of the West Philadelphia Community, which was headed by Nehemiah Davis and served over 300 homeless adults in Center City Philadelphia with a non-profit called Dare2Hope. It's a pretty awesome experience to serve others without expecting anything in return.

Being diagnosed with PTSD is challenging. Undergoing therapy and serving others, marked the turning point in regaining control of my life. At this point, I feel that I have arrived. What I mean by that is; I've built a base in my soul and I no longer feel like I'm less than any other human. I stopped allowing my insecurities and fear to dictate my potential. I'm building a satisfying career, an educational foundation and most of all, I am learning to enjoy my life. The world is new to me and not limited by the restrictive vision of anxiety.

CONCLUSION

In conclusion, thank you again for buying this book! We strongly believe this amazing book was able to offer you sufficient exposure & knowledge, which you inevitably need to STEER YOUR LIFE AND DESTINY IN THE RIGHT DIRECTION THROUGH THE MAGIC OF "FEARLESSNESS".

Knowing the impact that you are called to make in the world, even in great detail, is not enough for success. Another mission-critical piece is facing the fears, doubts, and mistaken beliefs that keep you from moving forward. Many of us carry subconscious ideals of what devoting oneself to a purpose-directed life would look like, such as living in poverty like Mother Teresa or separated from everyone you love serving in the Peace Corps.

These pictures trigger fears that living your higher purpose means sacrificing too much. In fact, the most paralyzing fears are the ones that lie deep within our subconscious, because we don't see them, and think something must be wrong with us if we aren't taking action toward our calling.

Imagine, instead of recognizing that you do have choice in how you express your calling. It makes such a difference when you realize that you can make specific commitments that will support you in your calling rather than suffer in service to an ideal.

Finally, if you enjoyed this book, then we'd like to ask you for a favor, would you be kind enought to leave a review for this book on Amazon? It'd be greatly appreciated! Click here to leave a review for this book on Amazon!

Thank you!

Made in the USA
Columbia, SC
06 January 2018